D1186559

FIFTY THRIFTY TIPS
for your
DREAM WEDDING

VICKY EDWARDS

summersdale

FIFTY THRIFTY TIPS FOR YOUR DREAM WEDDING

Copyright © Vicky Edwards, 2013

Illustrations © Shutterstock

Summersdale Publishers Ltd
46 West Street
Chichester
West Sussex
PO19 1RP
UK

www.summersdale.com

Printed and bound in the Czech Republic

ISBN: 978-1-84953-387-4

Substantial discounts on bulk quantities of Summersdale books are available to corporations, professional associations and other organisations. For details contact Nicky Douglas by telephone: +44 (0) 1243 756902, fax: +44 (0) 1243 786300 or email: nicky@summersdale.com.

For Stephanie Lawley, web guru
and beautiful bride-to-be

 # CONTENTS

Introduction...9

Organisation is the key.................................13

1. The Grand Plan
2. Boxing clever
3. Looks inviting
4. In the frame
5. Present days
6. Better to be safe…
7. Flower power
8. Nice day for a green wedding
9. Home or away?
10. In keeping with tradition

Pre-nuptials...37

11. Pre-wedding pamper
12. Just the two of us
13. Antler antics
14. Hooray for hens!
15. Guest services

Special appearances.......................................45

16. Dream themes
17. Wedding wardrobes: The bride

18. Wedding wardrobes: The groom's room

19. Wedding wardrobes: Bridesmaids, pages and
    matrons of honour

20. It's a gift

21. With this ring...

22. Bridal bling

23. Bride and groomed

24. Blooming gorgeous!

Location, location, location 65

25. Two into one WILL go

26. There's a place for us... somewhere

27. Fixtures, furniture and fittings

28. Hearts and flowers: Centrepieces

29. Deck the halls

30. Do me a favour

Standing on ceremony 81

31. Service sheets and signage

32. Wedding wheels

33. In tune

34. Throw, blow or wave: Confetti

Wed, fed and watered 91

35. How big a feast?

36. Catering clever

37. DIY dining

38. Cooking up a storm

39. To the bride and groom!
40. Called to the bar
41. Have your cake and eat it
42. Talking tables

Get the party started..109

43. A warm reception
44. Rave, revue or tea dance?
45. Child's play
46. Be our guest

Happily ever after..119

47. So long, farewell
48. And so to bed
49. Thank you very much
50. Host with the post

INTRODUCTION

Your wedding should be the happiest day of your life and planning it is exciting and fun. However, currently estimated at £21,000, for many couples the average cost of a wedding is as shocking as a best man's bluest joke. Certainly the prefix 'wedding' whacks up the cost of pretty much anything. Flowers, cake, dresses – put the 'W' word in front and the price escalates. But the day of your dreams is still attainable provided you tap into your resources, are prepared to negotiate and, above all, think creatively.

The golden rules you should keep at the forefront of your mind:

1. People love to help and to be involved in a wedding. If you have friends and family who can provide skills, services or time, ask them to do so. It really is that simple.

2. Once you know what your big day budget is, it is imperative that you and your intended have an honest conversation about your priorities. As a couple, what do you consider to be the most important elements of your wedding? Where are you willing to compromise, and what is non-negotiable? For instance, if you have always had your heart set on a big fairy-tale frock, then don't cheat yourself out of your dream dress, but be

open to cutting your budget elsewhere – for example, be more thrifty with expenditure on the cake, flowers, wedding cars, etc.

③ From favours to frocks and veils to vol-au-vents, it really is worth shopping around for *all* your wedding paraphernalia, as the difference can be considerable. Do research online suppliers as websites don't have the overheads of shops and so can usually offer more competitive prices. Likewise, you can probably save on delivery charges by giving local shops your custom.

④ If you don't ask, you don't get. Politely asking for a discount, whether in the form of money off, free delivery or an upgrade, can result in some spectacularly good deals. Paying cash can make a difference. Accepting and processing credit cards costs money and requires accounting so ask if there's any wriggle room for a cash transaction, especially when dealing with smaller traders. Similarly, if you're buying several items or services from the same supplier, then ask if there is anything that can be offered in exchange for a multiple order. As for upgrades, if you're getting married in the autumn or winter and you're looking at a hotel as your venue, check if they have more than one function room. If they do, see if they are willing to give you a bigger room for the same rate as the smaller room. If it's a quiet time of year, then they may be happy to give you a good deal in order to secure your booking. Think ahead and see the potential for negotiating. If you're uncomfortable asking for deals and discounts, then rehearse what you're going to say in advance. A few moments of courage could reap wonderful wedding rewards.

5 Finally, remember that some items on your wedding wish list can be acquired extremely cheaply from auction sites such as eBay, in charity shops, or through the small ads in your local paper. Better still, freebies from recycling sites such as Freecycle, which aim to reduce landfill by getting people to give away unwanted items, have turned up everything from cake stands to cufflinks for couples on a budget. All you have to do is send an email saying 'I do' in response to whatever is being offered.

Ultimately, this book is geared towards helping you to save money, at the same time as giving you inspiration and ideas to ensure that while your budget may be modest, your wedding will have bells on.

Good luck!

ORGANISATION IS THE KEY

♥♥♥♥♥♥♥♥♥

1 THE GRAND PLAN

Planning is absolutely critical when organising your wedding and the best way to ensure that you stay on track is to set up a spreadsheet or, if you're happier with a more 'old school' approach, a diary dedicated exclusively to the event.

Whichever you use, create a timeline within your planner and make a note of the dates by which each item and element must be booked, ordered, confirmed, paid for and/or collected. Ask to be notified when each delegated task has been completed, and if any glitches occur along the way, that you are told immediately. This buys you time to reorganise or reorder as required. Do make sure you dedicate a section to contact details, including telephone numbers, email and web addresses for all your suppliers and service providers, as well as anybody you are delegating jobs to. Make sure that your task force have contact information for anyone with whom they may need to liaise.

Get into the habit of checking your planner every day, even if you don't think you need to. Many a last-minute wedding crisis has been the result of details getting missed or people assuming that another member of the wedding party was taking care of something that in fact *nobody* had attended to. It is far better to double-check than to experience a single eleventh-hour moment of panic.

'Have nothing in your house that you do not know to be useful, or believe to be beautiful.'

So said William Morris, and in order to create your beautiful big day you'll definitely need something useful: a cardboard box.

Essentially, even if you're keeping track of everything with a spreadsheet or diary, you need a central hub in which to keep together samples, fabric swatches, magazine pages that you've torn out for reference, etc. Your 'Everything Wedding' box gives you a central hub for all your wedding planning bits and bobs. For example, rather than being in a blind panic three weeks down the line because you can't find that wine bottle label you tore off that had *exactly* the shade of blue you wanted for the bridesmaids' dresses, you'll know where to find it.

While your brain will be whirling with thoughts and inspirations, this humble box is going to be the physical storage for all your ideas in the run-up to your big day, so pick up a sturdy box at your local supermarket and decorate it with pretty paper, fabric or paint to transform it into something really special.

And then once you've tied the knot you'll have a beautiful box in which to store your wedding keepsakes. Ta-dah!

3 LOOKS INVITING

Look online for specialist wedding stationery companies, as they will almost certainly be able to undercut the high street suppliers. However, do also consider handmade invites, which have a truly personal feel. Another advantage of the handmade approach is that the cost really does come down. There are many computer programs and online tutorials for making invitations, including basic advice that will be a great help if IT isn't really your forte, and many of the DIY options can be printed out on a domestic printer. Visit websites like www.etsy.com for inspiration. One sure-fire way to save money on invites: proofread each one as you go. One bride of my acquaintance confesses that she had to reorder 160 invites, having beautifully handwritten them all, because she had made the same error on each one – her husband's name is Stuart Robert, not Stuart Rupert!

Some DIY invite ideas

 Character building

If you know a talented artist, ask them to sketch a caricature of you and your fiancé. Save the image and add it to any other wedding stationery.

Flash, bang, wallop!

Photoshop a photo of you and your betrothed, or perhaps a view that means something to you both – the setting of the proposal, for instance.

You are technically invited…

Alternatively, you could eliminate your postage costs by sending your finished invites by email, only printing out the invitations for guests who don't have access to email.

Face it

Create a Facebook page with your cover picture as your actual invite. Invite your guests to join the page to access their 'invite'.

Sewn up

Providing your wedding is going to be a fairly small affair you could, if you're skilled with a needle, embroider your invitations.

Cut 'n' paste

Scan newspaper supplements and magazines for pictures that match your theme or that might have special relevance to each of your guests. Glue onto card and hand-write the details.

To the letter

Simple to create but oh so striking, cut out letters from a newspaper and fix them to card.

Wedding wisdom

'I relied heavily on alternative wedding blogs and also Pinterest to inspire me. I spent a couple of hours each week scouring blogs for inspiration and creative ideas, which helped massively.'

Emily

4 IN THE FRAME

Almost everyone wants a pictorial record of their wedding day but if funds are tight, then as well as considering giving the job to a talented amateur photographer, ask all your friends and family to snap away, so you end up with a spontaneous and personal account of the day. Add a note to your invitees making it clear that you have no formal official photographer and that you would be grateful if people would bring their cameras and then email their snaps to you after the event. Add this request to your order of service, or ask the vicar or registrar to remind people by mentioning it again before the ceremony. Some of the best wedding shots are 'snaps' that have just been blessed with a little bit of luck as someone pressed the shutter. Another possibility is to check with local colleges and see if there is a photography course. A gifted student might well be willing to cover your wedding for a much smaller price tag as a means to getting some shots to kick-start their portfolio. However, you would have to accept that this option is not without risk. You could also explore the same idea with film students if you're keen to have a video recording of the day.

Perfect timing

If professional photography is a non-negotiable element, then shop around and consider the shots you really want.

If you're not too fussed about 'getting ready' shots, for example, then shorten the length of time you book your snapper for. Most photographers will have a scale of charges and packages based on the time they spend with you, so book professional shots of your day accordingly. Even with the buffer of an hour either side of the ceremony you should be able to cut your costs. But do make sure you ask lots of questions before you book anyone, including their training and experience and whether wedding photography is their main business strand (or do they specialise in something else)? Most importantly, check their reputation. Request testimonials or ask around and see what feedback you get.

Package deals

If you know you're going to be ordering a lot of shots, then it will almost certainly be to your advantage to purchase the full set and the rights to print them yourself. It may also be worth asking if your photographer offers a service whereby a couple of hours' editing tuition can be built into the deal. This gives you more scope with the shots you have, which could be especially beneficial if you have only had part of your day 'officially' photographed.

A photographic memory

Save on an album by making this yourself. A glue gun and a basic but sturdy album are the key tools for a physical photographic record, which you can of course decorate for a truly personal touch. But there are also many online options for creating a digital record. You could also consider uploading your pics to one of the many companies that will produce an album that you select the layout of yourself; you only order the finished article when you are entirely happy with your design. Whichever you choose, remember that even a basic album purchased through a photographer can be very expensive.

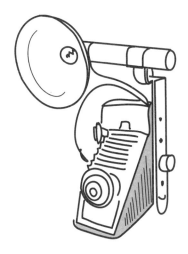

Wedding wisdom

'We found a cheaper wedding photographer by asking a lady who was in her first year in business as a professional. She agreed to a cheaper rate on the proviso that we would give her a good testimonial if we were happy with what she did. And we really were.'

Gavin

5 PRESENT DAYS

Asking for presents can be a tricky area. People like to give something to wish a couple well, and most would prefer to give something that will be genuinely useful and appreciated. The key is asking for what you want in such a way that your guests have a range of options in terms of cost and that doesn't make you sound too grasping – suggest that people club together to help spread the cost, for example. Etiquette suggests that asking for cash is 'not on', but for most modern couples, who have already set up home together, this can be the most practical and welcome solution. Done politely, asking for money is fine. But don't add the request directly to your invitation. Instead, add it to the insert (where you are likely to have transport information, etc.) and word it tactfully: *It is your presence and not your presents that we really want, but if you would like to give us a gift then we would be very glad of money towards a XXXX*. If people think they are donating towards something specific, they are less likely to mind being asked for money. Other thrifty gift ideas include:

Naturally gifted

Ask for your guests' skills as gifts. Know a photographer? Ask him or her to do your wedding pics. Your cousin is a hairdresser? Ask for wedding hair, not a wedding gift. An auntie who's a champion knitter? Get her to make you a fabulous blanket.

The Hit List

The traditional wedding list is a great option because you can give your guests an extensive range of differently priced items.

The gifts that keep on giving

Some people like to ask for donations to their favourite charity instead of gifts, which is a great way of supporting cash-strapped organisations. Ask your chosen charity for envelopes or donation details that can be included in your invites.

Vouchers-for-vows

If you're saving towards something particular, then ask for vouchers. Do make sure the company in question issues them in denominations as small as £5.00 and check the period of validity (some vouchers are only valid for a limited time).

Joined up

Memberships can make a great present and if you're keen on culture, natural history or have any other specific interests then you can always ask a group of pals to club together for membership to a specific attraction, gallery, club or 'friends' scheme.

6 BETTER TO BE SAFE...

Wedding insurance *can* save you money if, heaven forbid, anything should go wrong with your big day. However, before you start looking for wedding insurance take a good look at factors that might already cover you, up to a point. For example, did you know that if you pay for anything costing more than £100 (up to £30,000) with a credit card, that you can claim your money back from your credit card company? Section 75 of the Consumer Credit Act means that if there is a problem with goods or services that is deemed as a breach of contract, you should be able to recoup your loss – if your photographer didn't turn up, for example, or if your reception venue had been flooded and so was unable to accommodate your party. And if you have a home insurance policy, talk to the company concerned. Many insurers will cover key aspects of the big day for one month before and one month after the wedding.

If you decide to take out separate wedding insurance then do shop around, ask plenty of questions and read – and reread – the small print. There will almost certainly be exclusions and maximum cover limits. Consider, too, if you want to be covered for personal liability for injury to third parties or damage or loss to third-party property. There are policies that will cover the actions of all wedding guests, as well as the couple. You can also get cover for legal bills, personal accident and even counselling, if you have been severely stressed by wedding-related problems. If you are getting married abroad or are holding your ceremony and reception on different days, remember to check that the cover will still be effective.

7 FLOWER POWER

Even if you plan to do them yourself rather than booking a wedding florist, you should start thinking about flowers early on. One of the most common mistakes is for a bride to be absolutely set on a specific kind of flower. The changing seasons have a huge impact on what is readily available and therefore the price of the blooms. Floral flexibility is essential if you want to keep your costs down – but it certainly doesn't mean that you can't have glorious flowers. You just need to think in more general terms of the look and feel that you want.

Take the time to look at the flowers that are likely to be in season, and also to *smell* them. A beautiful bouquet or show-stopping arrangement ceases to appeal if the fragrance makes you feel nauseous or triggers a serious bout of hay fever.

Experiment with colour. Just because your bridesmaids' dresses are pink doesn't mean you have to go for pink roses. Look for colours that complement, and if you don't have an eye for colour, then ask someone whose judgement and style you trust and admire for advice.

One of the great things about flowers when you're on a budget is that very often less is more. Some of the most striking and beautiful arrangements are often the simplest: a single long-stemmed lily or a real red rose; a posy of daffodils in spring; arrangements of holly and ivy in winter.

Finally, if you are looking to book a florist, then shop around and book someone early on. Ask for recommendations and then, when you have appointed your florist, make use of their ideas and experience, don't just give them a wish list.

Top Tip!

Some of the most striking and beautiful arrangements are often the simplest.

8 NICE DAY FOR A GREEN WEDDING

Your wedding is an event that provides a great platform for your green credentials, and in many cases you can save time and money as well as the planet. Literally not costing the earth, an eco-wedding can become a thrifty wedding without actually having to try too hard.

Wedding webs

Keep your carbon footprint squeaky clean by setting up your own wedding website to act as a portal for the entire wedding party. You can include everything from photos to the gift list, and even the Bride's Blog.

IT for 'I do'

Communicate with guests by email or via a Facebook group. Reducing fuel miles, it will also save a fortune in postage.

Give me a ring

If you want a diamond engagement or wedding ring, then aim for one found from an ethical source or buy a fair trade ring. These are not the cheapest wedding bands, but then you'll be investing in a scheme that saves something far more significant than money. Alternatively, see if one of your female relations will part with a ring that they seldom wear; if it's not quite to your taste, you could have it remodelled at a fraction of the cost of buying new.

Spot on
Select a location that is as central as possible for your guests. Minimising travel for all saves money at a stroke.

The whole package
Choose suppliers who share your views and who use minimal packaging. In some instances you may even be able to negotiate discounts for purchasing goods without the packaging.

A snappy saving
Ask guests with digital cameras to share their photos online in a free Flickr (or similar) group instead of printing them. This saves using chemicals to print photographs, as well as the money it costs to do so.

'Hire' comes the bride
Hire your wedding dress. It's cheaper, more ecologically sound but still leaves you looking beautiful – what's not to like?

⑨ HOME OR AWAY?

If you don't mind having only a few friends and family members present when you get married, then tying the knot abroad can prove to be a very cost-effective way to wed. Many travel companies now specialise in wedding packages, very often with an in-resort wedding planner laid on for you as part of the deal, and these compare favourably with the price tag of a UK wedding. Currently Cyprus, Namibia, Sri Lanka, New York, Florida and Italy are among the most popular destinations for overseas weddings, with many couples opting for the wedding-and-honeymoon-in-one arrangement, followed by a big party back on home soil afterwards.

If this appeals, then do make sure that you do your homework, including a detailed check of the legalities of matrimony in the country in which you hope to marry, as it does differ depending where in the world you want to say 'I do'. To be certain about the rules and requirements your best bet, according to the UK Foreign Office, is to telephone the embassies in your preferred destination. Check practicalities such as whether or not your airline will allow you to take your wedding dress as hand luggage (you won't want it being bashed about in the hold), and bear in mind that you might also be required to obtain a Certificate of No Impediment (CNI) or a Nulla Osta (for marriages in Italy), which is a document that confirms that you are free to marry and that there is no other reason that prevents you from doing so. You also need to establish whether or not your marriage will be legally recognised in the UK. Advice from the UK Foreign Office suggests that you consult a lawyer to confirm that this is the case. You can find information, including details of foreign embassies, at www.fco.gov.uk.

Wedding wisdom

'The thought of spending £20,000 or more on one day, no matter how special, seemed ridiculous. So we did it abroad for £5,000. We had a wonderful time with our closest friends and family, then spent around £800 on a party for all our other friends at home. We got the best of both worlds.'

Alex

10 IN KEEPING WITH TRADITION

Weddings are rich in tradition and superstition. If this is important to you and your partner, then there are plenty of ways to incorporate these customs into your day, without having to pay too much for the privilege:

Something old. If any of your senior female relatives still has a wedding dress, then carefully unpick some of the fabric and tie it to your bouquet (a long sleeve is a perfect 'wrap' for a bouquet).

Something new costs nothing – your status as a newly-wed!

Something borrowed is an easy fix and make it anything you like.

Something blue can be achieved by attaching a simple blue ribbon to the underside of your dress.

The groom shouldn't see the bride the night before the wedding, according to superstition. Staying with a friend will almost certainly help quell any nerves more effectively than being alone in an (expensive) hotel room.

Chimney sweeps are meant to be a lucky omen at weddings – a pricey extra. If you know anyone who enjoys amateur dramatics, ask if they would 'play' a sweep instead.

Get married on a weekday. Although Saturday is still the most popular day for weddings, in the past it was thought unlucky. Nowadays, Saturday is the most expensive day to wed.

Horseshoes are lucky charms, popular as decorative items at weddings. Ask your local riding school or blacksmith if you can have some that have been consigned to the scrapheap. Spray them silver and use as table decorations.

PRE-NUPTIALS

♥♥♥♥♥♥♥♥

11 PRE-WEDDING PAMPER

A day at a spa getting 'match fit' is a lovely experience, but a costly one. If you really want to have a girly day then don't let your budget get in the way – just transform your home (or someone else's if space is a problem) into a DIY pamper paradise.

Invite your girlfriends along and ask each of them to bring a collection of lotions, potions, cosmetics and nail polishes, as well as a bath towel, a robe, and something delicious but healthy to eat – smoked salmon sandwiches, olives, strawberries, etc. Play soothing music and buy some cheap sparkling wine to make Buck's Fizz. Light scented candles, and when your guests arrive, invite everyone to pool their beauty products, change into their robes and then take it turns to give each other manicures, pedicures, facials and hairdos. Face packs are a must (and will make a wonderful photographic record!).

Alternatively, check with your local college to see if they run a hair and beauty course. If they do, you may be able to book your group in for a day that costs very little, as all the beauticians are trainees and people to practise on are usually very welcome.

12 JUST THE TWO OF US

Weddings can become all-consuming and a night alone with your beloved is worth setting time aside for – a 'pre-moon' to remind yourselves just why you're really doing this.

Instead of forking out top dollar for a hotel, why not have a really romantic night in, with candlelight, wine, soft music and an easily prepared but delicious dinner (some supermarkets do fantastic 'dine in' deals with wine thrown in)? Make it a 'No Wedding Talk Allowed' evening; just revel in each other's company. And who knows where the evening might lead.

Of course, there are some brilliant last-minute hotel deals that can be sourced from a range of voucher schemes that have sprung up in recent times. Sign up for alerts and keep your eye out for a cosy nook.

Finally, don't rule out your luck when it comes to bagging a break with your betrothed! If you jump on this idea in plenty of time, you can look for competitions where the prize is a hotel break. One bride entered so many wedding-related competitions that her prize haul not only netted her a night in a top London hotel, complete with a show and dinner, but also a set of silk wedding underwear and enough dry-cleaning vouchers to have her dress, her bridesmaids' dresses and also her mum's outfit professionally cleaned!

13 ANTLER ANTICS

In recent years the trend for OTT stag celebrations has escalated. Where once it was a few drinks in a pub or club with friends, today it's not unusual for these bashes to last several days and even entail leaving the country. This is definitely one area where you can make huge savings. Use your imagination – and give it free reign. Unless you're a stickler for tradition then your stag night really doesn't have to include lap dancers and kebabs.

Party like you stole it!

One of the best ways to have a reasonably priced stag party is to 'steal' an existing event or, to put it in less criminal terms, ride piggyback on it. Be it a music or arts festival (many are completely free), a sporting event or even – perish the thought! – a beer festival, by attaching your 'do' to an established event you take away a sizeable chunk of the planning, plus, by keeping the focus on one location, you'll spend less than you would on a pub-curry-club-casino type of bachelor jaunt. To find out what the options are at the time when you will be looking to party, check out your local tourist information service and local press. Have a shared fund for drinks and food or, if you're going to be somewhere where it's OK to picnic, arrange that each stag brings a different contribution. Be open-minded and don't dismiss something just because it doesn't appeal immediately. One groom admits that he had no idea that a steam festival could be such fun, although the abundance of cider and real ale tents may have played a part!

Hanging with my homies

Host the 'Boys' Big Night In' and really go to town. Cook up a huge curry (or order home delivery) and do whatever appeals – back-to-back viewings of *Star Wars* movies, a poker game, Xbox gaming, a DVD Race Night game or even something competitive and suitably daft like 'Chubby Bunnies' (who can fit the most marshmallows in their mouth and still say 'Chubby Bunnies' clearly). Kick back, embrace the theory that boys will be boys and save a packet while you're about it.

14 HOORAY FOR HENS!

Home is where the heart of the party is

If the thought of L-plates, Bacardi Breezers and a tour of local 'nite' clubs leaves you cold, relax; you can have a hen-tastic night that is as cheap, huge fun and, even better, that can be accomplished in your pyjamas. Yes, when it comes to hen dos, staying in is the new black, so invite your friends, snuggle into a brushed-cotton onesie and brace yourself for the ultimate sleepover!

Kick off the evening with an American-style supper, with each hen contributing a dish and a bottle. Entertainment is up to you, but you could watch movies (a bride who held an 'at home' hen party last year admits to back-to-back screenings of films including *Love Actually*, *Ghost*, *The Sound of Music* and *The Holiday*), play old-fashioned parlour games (charades, spin the bottle, truth or dare, etc.), get competitive on the Wii or the karaoke machine, or club together and hire a hot tub for the night so that you can lounge in bubbles while sipping a few too!

A midnight feast is compulsory, and it goes without saying that chocolate should feature heavily. You might fancy the idea of making your own cocktails (far cheaper than buying them in a club), or even starting your celebrations in the afternoon with a traditional tea party. If you're pushed for spare beds, ask the girls to bring their own blow-up mattresses and sleeping bags, so that when it's finally time to call it a night you all have somewhere to go and get your beauty sleep.

Live and learn

If you are set on going out, however, why not look at doing something that will leave you with a newly acquired skill, so you get far better value than you would from a night purely on the toot? From making shoes to dance lessons, book your hens in for an afternoon's (shared cost) activity followed by dinner in a bistro that allows you to bring your own booze in.

⑮ GUEST SERVICES

According to a March 2012 survey, the average cost of a wedding for each adult guest is approximately five hundred and ten pounds. Transport, accommodation, clothes, shoes, gifts – it all mounts up.

A way to help your nearest and dearest to make a saving is to really consider the location of your venue. You need somewhere with good transport links so that if people are coming by train they can easily make the return journey that same night, without having to pay for an overnight stay as well. Other things to bear in mind include: is there ample free parking available, or is your venue close to a park-and-ride scheme? Is it served by a local bus service, thus eliminating the need for the more expensive taxi journey (unless there are several people travelling together, in which case a cab may be cheaper)?

If overnight stays can't be avoided, call upon friends and family living close to your venue and ask if they will be willing to put people up for the night. If you are having a summer wedding, then ask those who are likely to be last on the dance floor anyway to bring a tent and see if local chums will supply a back garden as a temporary campsite with the use of their bathroom facilities. Some hotels will do a discounted rate for parties, so investigate in good time and see if you can secure a fixed price for your guests. Getting married out of term time? You may find that local colleges and universities have overnight accommodation that they will rent out reasonably cheaply.

SPECIAL
APPEARANCES

♥♥♥♥♥♥♥♥

16 DREAM THEMES

Themed weddings can be great fun but do be aware that they're not everyone's glass of Prosecco and specific themes involve hefty hire costs. Some people genuinely loath dressing up, so while you and your intended might adore all things *Star Wars*, being forced to embrace their inner Ewok might make your guests feel extremely uncomfortable (and not just because they'd be wearing a hot and hairy suit). A theme can, however, pull everything together and provide a framework to really give your wedding a 'Wow!' factor, and there are themes that give your guests a chance to participate without being out of their comfort zones and out of pocket.

Black and white is simple, stunning and is easily achieved by everyone.

Vintage is another fairly wide umbrella theme, leaving people free to dress in clothes from an era that they have a special fondness for and allowing for improvisation.

Colour coordinated means that while you give away the colour scheme of your wedding early on, you can ask guests to dress 'with a hint of pink/red/gold, etc.' to complement your chosen shades.

Movie stars leaves your guests to ponder on which big-screen legends they might secretly hanker after channelling. Wedding snaps featuring Marilyn Monroe, Laurel and Hardy, Shrek and Dumbledore are always fun, especially if you emphasise home-made, rather than hired, togs.

By the book, in a similar vein, invites a range of different options. Those who feel timid can opt to dress as more sedate characters from literature, while those who love a spot of dress-up can throw themselves into anything from Willy Wonka to Frankenstein!

Hats off is another relatively easily achieved theme, with guests just having to don their headgear of choice.

17 WEDDING WARDROBES: THE BRIDE

And the bride wore charity shop chic…

As well as sites like eBay, not to mention talented dressmakers amongst your friends and family, charity shops are a terrific resource for all sorts of wedding-related items. And there are those that also boast their own bridal departments, including a selection of beautiful wedding dresses (and suits for your chap). Oxfam, British Red Cross, Cancer Research and Barnardo's, for instance, all have bridal sections that sell brand new end-of-line dresses, donated by shops or designers. They also stock retro dresses, unearthed from Granny's attic, as well as dresses worn once and then gifted to the charity. Costs vary but for a new frock you can expect to pay roughly 30 per cent of what you would pay on the high street. This should leave you with enough in the budget to get your dress professionally fitted and altered and, if needs be, dry-cleaned. Shoes, accessories and bridesmaids' dresses are also often available too.

To find your nearest charity shops with bridal boutiques visit your favourite charity's website and search from there. Hopefully you will find your dream dress, but more than that, you will have the satisfaction of knowing that you are supporting a truly worthwhile cause. And let's face it: on a day that should be all about love, sharing that love with a charitable organisation has a decidedly harmonious feel to it.

Vintage or themed threads

As well as vintage dresses that you can find for sale in charity shops, hiring from your local theatre or dramatics society may also be an option. Check with them before you approach a big costume company, as these local resources may have a hire department of their own and the cost is likely to be lower than a mainstream costume-hire business.

A glimpse of stocking

A home-made garter is a pretty and fun finishing touch to your wedding ensemble and is a task that even the least adept seamstress can manage. Some brides like to incorporate a piece of lace from a family wedding dress, or perhaps add a detail such as a ring belonging to a mother, aunt or grandmother, which makes for a truly personal piece of bridal lingerie. You'll need lace, ribbon (two types; one of which should be wider than the other, sufficient to thread elastic through), elastic and beads/adornments. Look online for easy 'how to make' tutorials and get stitching.

18 WEDDING WARDROBES: THE GROOM'S ROOM

Getting shirty

An idea to consider for the groom and the male members of the wedding party is to keep the suit simple, but go all out on a fantastic shirt. For instance, most chaps can muster a plain black suit without having to buy one. With such a simple base, you can go for a very bright or patterned shirt in a good quality fabric. Buy rather than hire and don't rule out the high street, especially at sale time. Retail outlet parks also have the occasional wedding-garb gem. Alternatively, look at the possibility of something bespoke; buy the fabric and have shirts made to measure. If you're having several made, then you should have some negotiating power with a local tailor or seamstress, or even through the Internet. Prices do vary but you can have a shirt made to measure by an online supplier for under twenty pounds.

It's a tie

Another idea is to design your own ties. Head online where you can find companies who will help you to create customised wedding ties for as little as £6.99 each, allowing you to choose something absolutely unique.

Suits you

If you are looking to hire your suits, then it really does pay to shop around. Although online companies generally come out as more competitively priced (many deliver and collect the suits, too), the high street is still worth a visit as many suit-hire departments offer discounts if you're hiring suits for all the male members of the wedding party.

WEDDING WARDROBES: BRIDESMAIDS, PAGES AND MATRONS OF HONOUR

Question: When is a bridesmaid dress not a bridesmaid dress?

Answer: When it's just a dress.

♥ ♥ ♥

As long as you give yourself time to scout around then you will certainly find dresses for your bridesmaids that will look perfect without blowing your budget. The key is not to limit your search exclusively to bridesmaid dresses – once you know the colour you're after look at *all* dresses. This holds true of frocks for child bridesmaids and flower girls, older ladies and matrons of honour. Prom sections of department stores can very often yield what are essentially bridesmaid dresses but, because they don't have the prefix 'wedding', they are usually cheaper.

For baby and child attendants second hand is also a highly cost-effective option. Children grow so fast that second-hand wedding attire has most likely only ever been worn once and so should still be in mint condition. One bride reports kitting all six of her small attendants out in beautiful silk outfits purchased on eBay for less than the cost of a single department store dress, selling them again after the wedding and making back almost exactly what she had spent in the first place. Local newspaper small ads are also good hunting ground for little people's togs.

20 IT'S A GIFT

Buying gifts for your attendants is a tricky one as the chances are you will have a disparate collection of tastes and age ranges to cater for. But there are some really thoughtful, personal and inexpensive 'thank you' presents available.

- Paint a mug at a pottery cafe and personalise it with a message and the date. Choose mugs to suit each person – a pint pot for the best man, a small and delicate cup and saucer for the mums or bridesmaids and a small child's beaker for your little attendants.

- Vintage books make lovely gifts and if you set aside the time to trawl local flea markets, second-hand bookshops and the Internet, then you will find books with titles that fit the occasion. Write a heartfelt note inside the cover.

- An inexpensive but thoughtful gift for the ladies in your party is a pair of pretty flip-flops – perfect for when they want to ditch their high heels and hit the dance floor!

- A home-baked cake or home-made jam or chutney, finished with a special wedding label and beautifully wrapped, is a true labour of love.

If you can sew, knit or crochet, make small bride and groom rag dolls for little flower girls and ring bearers.

Paint old jars with glass paints and fill them with sweeties or soaps.

Vintage glasses can be purchased second hand very cheaply. Choose pretty or interesting ones and present them with a small bottle of wine.

Go to a craft shop and stock up on jewellery-making materials. Make bracelets for the ladies and cufflinks for the men.

Wedding wisdom

'My mum married during the war so it had to be the thought that counted because money was very tight. She wrote her bridesmaids' letters, telling them how she valued their friendship. Later she pressed some flowers from her bouquet for them.'

Jaine

21 WITH THIS RING...

On your metal

When it comes to saving money on your wedding rings, your best option is to ditch the traditional platinum or gold rings in favour of a less precious but nevertheless hard-wearing metal. Rings made from titanium, palladium and even tungsten are growing in popularity – and the difference in price is significant. A platinum ring costing almost £500 could be replaced with a titanium or tungsten ring costing just eighty pounds. Better still, these less traditional metals last just as well as their more precious cousins. And if you particularly wanted diamonds or another type of stone set in your wedding ring then it should still be possible with most of the cheaper metals, and of course, if you've saved on the metal, that should free up some cash for additional sparkle! Many high street jewellers do not sell a wide range of alternative metal rings (if any), so the Internet really is your best starting point.

Hand-crafted for your fingers

Although bespoke rings might imply a hefty price tag, local craftspeople or those who sell their wares through sites like Etsy may surprise you with their competitive prices. And, of course, you'll have something absolutely unique. Set aside time to really shop around and explore your options.

Seconds out

If the idea of a second-hand ring doesn't bother you, then there will always be bargains to be had. Make it 'yours' by having it engraved with a message or phrase close to your heart.

Top Tip!

Ditch the traditional platinum or gold rings in favour of a less precious but nevertheless hard-wearing metal.

22 BRIDAL BLING

Something old meets something new with a beautiful piece of handmade bridal vintage jewellery that you can conjure yourself in a matter of minutes for a fraction of the cost of something shop bought. Ask your older relatives if they have a brooch that they would donate, or perhaps you already have something suitable lurking at the back of your jewellery box, even something that belonged to a special female relative who is no longer here. Research ways of adapting an existing brooch or pendant into a statement piece for your wedding.

- Second-hand shops, vintage and antiques shops, car boot fairs and even jumble sales can all be marvellous sources for unique 'budget bling'.

- Try a local craft shop for pretty beads and make yourself something unique. You could even make matching jewellery for your bridesmaids.

- Ticking off something borrowed, ask someone close to lend you something in the baubles, bangles and beads department.

- If you have a small charm or locket from your childhood that has sentimental value, stitch it to your dress.

- Look online for one-off pieces that are both unique and affordable. Sites like folksy.com can turn up some exquisite pieces.

- Tiaras do set off a wedding gown beautifully, but they can be a costly addition, ranging from £50 upwards, new. Try auction sites where you will find them much cheaper. Do make sure you look carefully at the picture, ask questions if you're not able to see the smaller details and check the returns policy in the event that you're not satisfied.

- You can also make your own tiara, headband or fascinator. A quick search online will lead you to several tutorials, so if you fancy a go at making your own headgear then take a look. This way you'll save money and also have a special wedding heirloom to pass on.

23 BRIDE AND GROOMED

Every bride wants to look her best on her big day, but the services of professional hairdressers and make-up artists add to your overall spend. One option is to do your own hair and make-up, but unless you are confident of being able to achieve the exact look you're after, then you might want to ask for help. The most obvious solution is to ask a friend with skills in this area, but if this doesn't yield any results then think about acquiring some skills…

Teach yourself gorgeous!

Once again, the Internet is a veritable hub of brilliant ideas and tutorials, so if your eyeliner always goes on wonky, or you just can't manage a neat chignon, then find a demonstration and try, try and try again.

Here come the girls

Most department stores and major chemists have a range of premium brand cosmetic counters, each staffed by sales people who will gladly demonstrate their products on you. You don't have to buy anything, but do take the free advice – and very often handy free samples!

Doubly talented

Ask your make-up artist if she is able to do a simple 'up' do for you. Most beauticians will have completed some sort of basic hairdressing course as part of their studies and if the hairdo you're hoping to achieve is relatively simple then she may be willing to give you a deal on doing both hair and make-up.

Time for a trim

There's cutting costs and there's cutting corners. Grooms should NOT pay a visit to the barber too close to the wedding date. If you're going to have a close shave and/or a trim, make sure you have enough time to let any cuts, shaving rashes and potentially 'too short' crops recover.

24 BLOOMING GORGEOUS!

A bride's bouquet is very much a matter of personal taste, but try to keep a relatively open mind; decide what sort of size and shape you would like your bouquet to be, but before you go any further, take a good look at what is going to be in season when you marry. If you plan to use a florist, then take advice on in-season flowers, which will help to reduce the price tag. If you're planning to buy the blooms and then create your bouquet yourself (or someone else is doing this for you), buy wholesale from flower markets or nurseries and use simple ideas for your bouquet; a hand-tied cluster of flowers, for example. Make sure you select flowers that are robust and that will still look as fresh at the end of the day as they did at the start.

Another idea is to pick your own. If you can count keen gardeners amongst your acquaintances, see if any are likely to have anything blooming at the time of your wedding and if so, they might let you take your pick – literally! – for your bouquet and buttonholes.

Finally, if the idea of traditional carnation-and-fern buttonholes and corsages doesn't appeal, why not consider silk flowers? Giving you a broader choice, these can be purchased cheaply from garden centres, lifestyle stores and even from your local high street discount store. These wonderful floral fakes can be easily fashioned into a stunning wedding accessory.

LOCATION, LOCATION, LOCATION

♥♥♥♥♥♥♥♥♥

25 TWO INTO ONE WILL GO

Unless you are set on a church wedding then a venue that can accommodate both your marriage service and the reception may prove to be a cost-effective option. Eliminating the transport costs – not to mention the time and logistical problems – between venues, hotels, wedding barns, theatres and other licensed venues with space to accommodate the 'after' party too are worth investigating. Your local registrar will have an up-to-date list of all the venues nearby.

As far as hotels go, don't rule out the smaller and seemingly less fancy ones. One couple wed at an airport-based hotel, which not only proved a total bargain, but also meant the swiftest getaway the next day when they departed for the honeymoon – straight out of the hotel entrance and onto an airport courtesy bus! Used predominately for the ease of travellers with early flights to catch, the hotel still had a good-sized function room that, apart from the occasional business meeting, didn't get much action. Delighted to host a wedding, the hotel couldn't have been more helpful and, most importantly, more reasonably priced. Keep an open mind and even if the venues on the list don't have instant appeal on paper, go and see them and talk to staff about how they might help you achieve your perfect wedding.

And if you *do* have your heart set on a church wedding, see if the church hall can be incorporated into a package, once again giving you both service and reception on the same site.

Top Tip!

A venue that can accommodate both your marriage service and the reception may prove to be a cost-effective option.

26 THERE'S A PLACE FOR US... SOMEWHERE

If you do opt for separate venues for the ceremony and the reception, then one of the best blank canvases for your 'after party' is your local scout hut, parish centre or village hall. Many buildings were renovated as part of the millennium celebrations, or more recently the Diamond Jubilee celebrations, and so now look great and boast all mod cons. Another advantage of community halls is that they tend to have parking on site. They also often boast some sort of garden area, which allows you to let the sun in if your wedding day is fine, but also offer swiftly found shelter should the heavens throw down watery confetti.

If you're looking for a hall that requires less decorating, check out your local Masonic hall. Many of these are available for private hire and are generally very well decorated and maintained, and again, a cheaper option than, say, a hotel.

Other possible venues to consider:

- **Barns** – and not just the ones marketed as wedding reception venues. Speak to local farmers and see if they do – or would consider – private hire.

- **Local restaurants, hotels or pubs** – look at those with function rooms or private dining rooms (or even exclusive hire, which isn't always as pricey as you might imagine, depending on the day of the week you are marrying).

- **Picnic spots** – If you can guarantee the weather (or are feeling brave), then an al fresco reception is certainly cheap. But you will need to consider lavatory facilities and parking arrangements.

- **Marquee hire** – Although the initial hire fee may provoke a sharp intake of breath, bear in mind that so long as you have a suitable plot for it, a marquee means that you can self-cater, which will, of course, save you money.

- **Local schools and colleges** – especially private institutions, have either rooms for hire or grounds upon which you can pitch a marquee. Because this isn't their main revenue stream, or what they are fundamentally known for, you may find that you can negotiate a good deal.

27 FIXTURES, FURNITURE AND FITTINGS

If you're hiring a hall or room then you may find that you need to provide certain fixtures, furniture and fittings yourself; anything from tables and chairs to loo rolls and washing-up liquid. Make sure that when you view potential venues you ask for a precise inventory of what is included in the package and, perhaps more importantly, what is not. Check how many power points there are in the room, what kind of heating or air-conditioning is available, where the fuse box is and what kind of back-up is in place in the event of a power cut.

If you need tables and chairs, then ask local schools or colleges if they have a hire agreement in place. You may well be able to secure all you need for a one-off fee, providing you collect and deliver items (and instead of expensive chair covers, experiment with florist's ribbon and netting bought wholesale from a fabric warehouse). Or, consider borrowing wallpaper pasting tables from friends and family. These are big enough to seat several people and can easily be covered by a tablecloth.

If the lighting is not conducive to a party atmosphere (fluorescent tubes won't flatter even the most beautiful bride), ask if you can cover them with more ambient tinted sleeves (available online), or see if candles are permitted so that you can reduce the amount of overhead lighting.

Crockery and cutlery hire can be saved on by borrowing like crazy! Mismatched vintage china looks stunning, so start asking everyone you know for a loan of their prettiest pieces.

28 HEARTS AND FLOWERS: CENTREPIECES

Fresh flowers are beautiful, but undeniably expensive. However, tissue paper and other craft materials, comparatively, are not. Even if you are not the most naturally gifted person in the world when it comes to crafts, rest assured that there are lots of ways to DIY your centrepieces without breaking the bank or your spirit.

If you know anyone who is a dab hand at origami, then now is the time to put their paper creativity to the test and get them to help you make something special (primary school teachers are usually a good bet!).

Hit the Internet. A quick search soon delivers you step-by-step instructions for making all types of flowers in all manner of shapes, sizes and forms. You can even add in ribbons and fabric for added texture and detail.

Make big blooms from newspaper (the *Financial Times* ties in beautifully with a pink colour scheme) and create table decorations that won't so much make headlines as be the headlines!

Glue tissue paper fashioned into rosebuds to twigs (collected on walks) and display in simple glass vases or painted jam jars.

But if you're adamant that it has to be the real deal, think about:

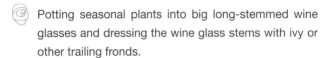 Potting seasonal plants into big long-stemmed wine glasses and dressing the wine glass stems with ivy or other trailing fronds.

Going with the seasons: use catkins, pussy willow, blossom, summer roses or holly. Use a deep bowl and cover the surface in a criss-cross grid of sticky tape. Fill with water and drop the stems through the grid for a professional look at a home-made price.

Wedding wisdom

'I saw a fantastic window display of different coloured cabbage roses, all made out of tissue paper. It turned out that the shop owner's husband was the paper rose genius so when my man proposed, I went back to the shop and asked how to make them so that I could decorate the pew ends in church and make some special centrepieces. The results, which cost next to nothing, won me loads of compliments.'

Martina

29 DECK THE HALLS

From rustic charm to Masonic splendour, hiring a hall and 'dressing' it can provide the perfect reception venue.

While venues for ceremonies are limited to those licensed for weddings and partnership ceremonies, the reception venue offers you far greater scope and even the most unlikely venue can be temporarily transformed into a wedding wonderland with cheap but clever decoration and a bit of careful set dressing; marquee companies can provide drapes, swags and bows to dress a room, for a fraction of the cost of hiring a marquee. Or, if you've got the confidence to give it a go yourself you can buy muslin, gauze and netting very reasonably from fabric wholesalers. Remember! If you're not enamoured with the interior of a room or hall, try to look beyond the physical space and to see the potential. Just as a figure-flattering frock can make a difference to a lady with big hips, so can artfully hung drapes and a bit of bling transform the WI's meeting room.

Never underestimate the power of bunting! Some brides have even included bunting making in their hen party celebrations, with each 'hen' making a few triangles to add to the celebratory line of flags. Bunting strung across a room immediately gives a fiesta feel to even the drabbest space.

If you don't have time or inclination to sew, doily bunting is a brilliant cheat and looks stunning. Coloured doilies (so cheap in high street bargain shops) folded in half and stapled to ribbon look amazing.

Home-made banners can look striking and can mask off areas that aren't so easy on the eye. If you have artistic chums, ask them to transform three or four cheap sheets into works of art that fit your theme. One groom and his pals created a brilliant cartoon-inspired story of his and his fiancée's relationship to the altar using stick men and speech bubbles. Simple, but striking and a fantastic talking point, it also hid an ugly wall.

Depending on the electricity available to you, fairy lights and lanterns are an easy way to transform the look of a room. But make sure you get someone who knows what they are doing to advise you so that your requirements are safe.

Photo displays of the happy couple lend a very personal touch and look fabulous.

Carefully used and artfully arranged twigs, fir cones and foliage can look very effective and are free if you snip from friends and neighbours and (discreetly!) from trees and hedgerows on public footpaths and bridleways.

Wedding wisdom

'I filled small glass vases with sweet peas as table decorations, interspersing them with tea lights and scattered rose petals. They looked beautiful.'

Jacqueline

㉚ DO ME A FAVOUR

The customary wedding favour offered to guests is five sugared almonds, but the days of this teeth-breaking confectionary are numbered. Modern couples are increasingly breaking with tradition, instead offering a marriage memento that is more personal, topical, inspired or economical.

You've been lucky in love so try to get your good fortune to rub off on your guests. Pop a lottery ticket or scratch card into a decorated envelope and add a personal note expressing the sentiment. At just one pound per head, the cost is on a par with the more traditional favours – but you could make someone a millionaire!

If you've got poetic tendencies, then a thoughtful but economical option is to give each guest a copy of a poem that you have written about your thoughts on your marriage and your wedding, including something about how important it is that each of your guests are there. Roll into a scroll and tie with ribbon, lace or string.

Let love grow! A packet of sunflower seeds presented in a mini terracotta pot is a lovely keepsake for your guests. Paint their names on the pots for a personal touch.

If you're from a family of knitters, why not use old bits of leftover wool in neutral colours to knit mini brides and grooms or lucky horseshoes for each of your guests?

If you support a particular charity, brooches such as the various cancer ribbons or the British Heart Foundation silk lapel rose make original favours. Furthermore, your purchase contributes to a worthwhile cause. Visit your favourite charity's website for details.

STANDING ON CEREMONY

♥♥♥♥♥♥♥♥♥

SERVICE SHEETS AND SIGNAGE

If you are having an order of service or song sheet, then make sure you get maximum use from it. For instance, is there room on the back to reiterate the directions to the reception? Signage at your reception is also extremely useful for your guests – present drop-off, toilets, cloakroom, bar, parking, etc. A great way to keep costs down is to create these elements yourself.

Orders of service

Design these yourself (to tie in with your invitations, if you wish) and then get them printed professionally (online or local printers will be your best bet), or buy good quality paper/card and print them on a domestic printer. An idea that offers a pretty touch is to roll rather than fold your finished article and then tie it, like a scroll, with ribbon or string.

Signage

You can either design and print these in the same way as your order of service, or another fun and thrifty way to point people in the right direction is to buy A4-sized blackboards and either drill holes in them and hang them in the appropriate places, or prop them up where they are needed. You could also use empty picture or mirror frames (often available very cheaply in junk shops) into which you can pop a handwritten direction.

The case continues

Instead of buying a purpose-made box for people to deposit cards in, take a trip into Granny's attic or have a root around a local junk shop and unearth a vintage suitcase. Line it with pretty fabric or handmade paper and dress it with ribbons, and you will have made a beautiful drop-off point for cards, vouchers and cheques. When open, add a sign to the inside of the case lid upon which you can write something along the lines of: 'Cards and paper gifts here, please.' Or if Granny can't rustle up a suitcase, see if she can unearth an old-fashioned bird cage, a hat box or an old instrument case instead.

Wedding wisdom

'Our wedding was beach-themed so we used bits of driftwood for signs by just painting the words on with white paint. We threaded twine through and hung them. They looked really great.'

Felicity

③② WEDDING WHEELS

Transport is an area where huge savings can be made. Sure, it's lovely to have a fleet of vintage cars or a horse and carriage to take you to your wedding, but unless you are extremely lucky to have friends in the trade, or with jolly swanky cars, the expense is a big one.

Depending on how far you need to travel, consider your local taxi firm. Many have minibuses as part of their fleet, which should have enough space to accommodate the immediate wedding party, with the bride and whoever is giving her away following in a separate car.

If you long for horse power, talk to local stables and see if they can help rather than approaching a wedding specialist horse-drawn carriage company, but do bear in mind that there may be issues regarding personal insurance to be considered.

One of the cheapest ways to get to your wedding without compromising too much on style is simply to ask friends with smart looking cars to make their wedding present to you both to chauffer you and your party in their own vehicles. For a 'proper' wedding car touch you can always tie streamers to the cars.

Finally, if it isn't far to your venue (and providing you have a big umbrella just in case!) do as they did in the old days and promenade to the altar.

Wedding wisdom

'The Morris Minor used for the bridesmaids was down to my mum having a conversation with Alex's girlfriend's mum who had a friend with a Morris Minor. The Power of Mum Gossip is brilliant!'

Emily

33 IN TUNE

If music be the food of *your* love, then you'll want to include it in your ceremony. One thing that you absolutely must check when you book your ceremony is if it is possible to have live music there – some venues simply offer a CD player or MP3 player for you to use. If this suits your purpose, great. However, if live music is a really important part of the marriage ceremony for you then you'll need to be sure that you can achieve this.

Hiring musicians to play or sing at your service is an added extra to your budget, so tap into the talents of your friends and family. Ask any singers or musicians to perform something that has some special resonance for you and your beloved. Alternatively, ask your local music college if they have anyone who might be willing to do something for the experience at a reduced fee.

Another alternative is just to print the lyrics of a well-known 'happy' song on your order of service and get someone with a good tuneful voice to start everyone off and lead them in song at the very end of the service. 'Bring Me Sunshine', synonymous with Morecambe & Wise, is a delightfully cheerful 'all sing' wedding number.

Remember, the registrar or vicar will have to approve your music choices, so don't pick anything too outlandish. In a secular ceremony you won't be permitted to have hymns or anything that references religion, so again, think through your choices carefully.

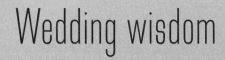

Wedding wisdom

'My seven-year-old niece played "Love Me Tender"
on the recorder while we signed the register. It might
not have been note perfect but it was really
personal and everyone loved it.'

Victoria

34 THROW, BLOW OR WAVE: CONFETTI

Many venues take a dim view of confetti these days. Even the recycled paper version leaves a mess, which, especially for town centre venues, is tantamount to littering. While keeping the tradition (throwing seed, rice or confetti originates in the theory that it was an act that promoted fertility and kept evil spirits at bay) but dispensing with the mess, here are some alternative suggestions for things to 'throw' at the happy couple – but remember to throw with care! Some of the ideas suggested below could leave a pair of newly-weds bruised rather than blissed out! And make sure you make your wishes for confetti known on your invite.

- Dried rose petals. Ask all your friends to collect them from their gardens and then dry them and fill small paper bags with them. Ask your ushers to hand them out before the ceremony starts. Other ideas could include birdseed, rice, dried lavender or popcorn.

- Another thought is to 'blow' or 'wave' rather than 'throw'. For instance, kids' bubble-blowing pots and wands can be bought really cheaply from supermarkets and, when blown en masse, the bubbles make a beautiful sight and a terrific photo opportunity. Do take care not to target the bridal gown, though, as the cheap soap might stain.

Sparklers are also another pretty nod to tradition but far less messy. Remember to put someone in charge of lighters or matches and health and safety issues, such as making sure that kids are supervised.

Balloons in colours that complement your theme can be tied to each chair in your ceremony room. At the end of the service ask guests to untie their balloons and form a guard of honour with them.

WED, FED AND WATERED

♥♥♥♥♥♥♥♥♥

35 HOW BIG A FEAST?

Much of how you plan your catering depends on how many sets of guests you are inviting. If you are inviting one set to the ceremony and the wedding breakfast, followed by an evening guest list for the party, you will probably want to offer at least a snack to your second group of arrivals.

The question of how many courses arises for your first feast. Traditionally, there are three courses, followed by cake and coffee, but it's better to be led by your budget rather than tradition, so think about what best suits your needs, then factor in the time of day you are marrying. If you will be sitting down to eat at noon, for instance, you will want to serve something reasonably substantial.

There is nothing to say that you can't serve your cake as the pudding option and, providing you have given people a sturdy starter and main course, it's unlikely that anyone will go hungry.

Remember, food doesn't have to be fancy to be delicious and attractively served. If you're hiring caterers or have a hotel team looking after your menu, consider dishes that are filling and that can be easily adapted for vegetarians or vegans.

For your evening celebrations, make sure that guests know in advance what level of catering to expect. You don't want people turning up hungry, anticipating a hog roast and finding nothing more than crisps and bar nuts. It's OK to spell it out in your invite:

Please come and join us for drinks and canapés. (Please note that there is a pay bar.)

36 CATERING CLEVER

If you know that catering your wedding yourself is a stretch too far, then you will need to rely on a good caterer. If you're using a hotel or restaurant, then you will be obliged to use their team, but that doesn't mean you can't negotiate so that you have what you want. They may well have standard menu options from which to choose, but most chefs will be prepared to adapt to suit your specific requirements. Be clear about what you want and if you're not sure, ask their advice. They will know well which dishes are most popular, more economical, easiest to adapt for specific dietary needs, etc. Insist on sampling the proposed menu so that you can approve it.

If you are going to use an outside caterer, then the same rules apply, although you can opt to use them for just part of your feast. If you know that your mum makes a wicked pudding, and that she's happy to do so, make it clear that you don't want your caterer to do this and expect it to be reflected in the cost. Likewise, if you want to use fresh bread, cheese or indeed anything else from a particular local supplier, deal directly with them and ask your caterer simply to serve it.

The best way to find a good caterer is through personal recommendation, but if this isn't possible then do ask for references and meet with prospective candidates for the job. Go armed with a comprehensive list of questions, including a request for detailed costings so that you know exactly what you can expect for your money. And don't overlook smaller companies who operate from small units; lower overheads probably mean lower prices.

37 DIY DINING

Increasingly popular is the bring-your-own wedding feast. Just like an American-style supper, ask people to bring something to contribute to the feast, capitalising on your guests' unique culinary expertise. Be specific; you don't want 50 bowls of salad but not a carb in sight, so if you are going the BYO route then flag it up clearly on your initial invite, followed by a request for a specific item (if you know Auntie makes an apple pie to die for, ask her to make a couple). You might want to offer part of the feast – cold meats, cheese, salads and bread, say – and to ask guests to bring the extras.

The traditional cold buffet type of picnic, if you have friends and family who are willing and able, is a popular staple of weddings. If you can rely on a team who will each contribute to this British version of the smorgasbord, and you can factor in things like cold storage and setting it up on the day, then this can be one of the most cost-effective ways of catering your wedding.

Another clever way to cut the cost is to keep the picnic food very simple. Ploughman's lunches are another easy option, with cheese and cold meats on offer to cater for carnivores and veggies alike.

Alternatively, you can just ask everyone to bring their own picnic and then simply supply rugs or tables – and a knock-out pudding!

Wedding wisdom

'Instead of a big wedding cake, we chose to have a wedding cake table – friends who enjoy baking offered to make a tasty treat for the table which added up to a great mix of cakes and puddings.'

Emily

38 COOKING UP A STORM

Menus, whether DIY or catered, need to be considered carefully. Seasonal fruit and veg, for instance, will be cheaper, but you also need to think about practicalities. If your feast is taking place in a venue with limited kitchen facilities, then a cold spread may work best for you. With a well-equipped kitchen at your disposal, however, you can be much more creative.

- Home-made shepherd's pies, curries or chilli can be cooked in huge batches and then frozen until needed by willing volunteers. Then you just need a team to coordinate the heating and serving on the day.

- Hog roasts are filling and delicious, so a hog roast company may be worth exploring. It's a great option if you have a guest list of carnivores!

- Similarly, a fish-and-chip van may not work out as an overly expensive option and can be a really fun way to tuck in.

- If marrying in summer, then a barbeque may fit your requirements – but you do need a couple of keen and expert barbie chefs to make sure this runs smoothly, as well as access to mass catering oil drum-style barbeques. Talk to your local butcher about costs for bulk-buying sausages and burgers.

Having an afternoon reception? High tea is a pretty and popular choice – delicate sandwiches, scones with jam and cream and of course oodles of cake! Asking friends to bring some home-made contributions will help keep costs down.

At a winter reception a steaming home-made hearty broth can be a fantastic meal in itself. Serve with generous wedges of crusty bread and lashings of butter.

Real men may not eat quiche, but wedding guests do! Find the quiche queen in your circle and ask them to cook as many as you need. Serve with a simple salad, good quality bread and coleslaw.

Wedding wisdom

'My sister catered our wedding, making huge doorstep sandwiches from lovely rustic bread filled with roast beef, cheese and pickle and tuna, and serving them with just three types of salad.'

Michelle

39 TO THE BRIDE AND GROOM!

No wedding is complete without a toast to the happy couple (and then maybe a few more glasses, just to be sure!). If you're in the hands of a hotel or restaurant for your wine and champagne, then open negotiations with the resident sommelier early on to get the best possible deal. You may be able to supply your own wine, but expect to pay corkage, which may negate any saving.

As to the toasts, remember that sparkling wine has come a long way in recent years and unless you are a connoisseur you'd be pushed to tell it apart from champagne – but for the price.

If you are self-catering, then you have greater scope for reducing the bar bill. If you're a keen brewer or winemaker, then consider making your own home concoction as a part of your wedding's liquid cheer. A punch or Buck's Fizz (made with sparkling wine) makes a good welcome drink and there are always supermarkets and off-licences with special deals on wine and beer.

If cider and beer are to feature on your tipple menu, then contact your local independent brewery and look at purchasing direct from them. They may be able to offer you a discounted price for ordering a full barrel and may be willing to give you the same discount as they offer to pubs. Alternatively, you could ask your friendly local publican to order on your behalf.

Finally, remember to cater for non-drinkers and those who will, at some point in the day at least, be glad of a nice cup of tea.

Top Tip!

Remember to cater for non-drinkers.

40 CALLED TO THE BAR

It's all very well providing the booze for your celebrations, but if you're hosting your own reception then you will need someone to take on the role of head barman (or woman). If you are operating a free bar, then see if a couple of mates will run it for you, but if you're on good terms with your local pub you could ask if they will supply both the booze and someone to take care of the bar for you. You will, of course, have to pay them, but you'll be getting someone experienced who can run this area with ease and efficiency for you. If you want to operate a pay bar from unlicensed premises, then you will have to apply to the local authority (usually the district council) for a Temporary Event Notice. Allow plenty of time to investigate this option.

Another option is to ask a friend with a flair for cocktail making to do a couple of hours in the evening of shaking and stirring. See if they can create a couple of appropriately named wedding cocktails – Paradise, White Lady or a Screaming Orgasm, perhaps? Buying the ingredients wholesale will save you money, so ask around and see if you can find someone you know with access to a cash and carry card.

If you are hosting your 'after party' at a venue that has its own bar, then plan ahead and decide how much money you are going to put behind the bar for free drinks for your guests – and stick to it. Once again, make it clear on your invite what the arrangements are so that your guests can plan accordingly.

41 HAVE YOUR CAKE AND EAT IT

A professionally made wedding cake is expensive so unless you have a pro cake maker in your midst you will need to look at alternatives in order to cut your costs as well as your cake. You also need to plan ahead. If you are making a fruit cake, for example, make sure it has time to mature nicely. If you are ordering a cake, then consider practicalities such as collection and transportation to the reception venue and if it will need refrigerating.

Ice, ice baby

Making your own is one option. If you're no good with an icing bag, then ask someone who is to do the decorative bit.

Say cheese

Combine the cheese and biscuits course of your wedding breakfast with your wedding cake. Build your own cake, in exactly the same style as a traditional tiered wedding cake, using different (whole) cheeses. You can have as many tiers as you like for your fabulous *fromage* tower!

Buy it off the shelf

If you're keen to have a traditional wedding cake but aren't so eager to bake it yourself, several supermarkets now sell plain white-iced cakes. You could even use your supermarket club card points to pay for it.

The Great Bridal Bake Off

If you're not fussed about tradition, then the world is your sponge-based oyster. Home-baked cupcakes, fairy cakes, mini Victoria sponges or even brownies look fantastic when artfully arranged.

Seasonal cakes

If you are marrying at a specific time of year, tie the season in: chocolate or simnel cake for an Easter wedding, pavlova nests filled with seasonal strawberries for a summer union, or even an elaborate apple pie for autumn.

Fun with fondue

A chocolate fondue is an unusual alternative to a traditional cake. See if you can borrow two or three fondue sets and involve your guests in creating this choccy delicacy. Serve with plates of fruit, shortbread, wafers, marshmallows and nuts to dip into the goo.

Joined in jelly

Jelly is back in style and there are lots of fun moulds available now. Cheap and easy to make, a layered jelly served with ice cream makes a retro cake alternative.

Cheat's eats

Naughty but most definitely thrifty, do as one couple did and have a theatrical prop cake on display. Be photographed with the imposter cake, knife poised, and then whip it away out of sight. Present your guests with slices of a far cheaper cake that have been pre-cut!

Wedding wisdom

'I used a Christmas cake recipe. I had the smallest size cake tin, and hired the two larger ones. Made well in advance, a few days before the wedding, I covered the cakes with marzipan and icing. On the wedding day, I simply placed one cake on top of the other and added my decorations.'

Jacqueline

42 TALKING TABLES

From place settings to seating plans, there are lots of ways to give your tables (thrifty) pizzazz.

Looking like a lemon

A really cheap but effective centrepiece for tables is a large glass vase filled with lemons or limes and green foliage. Simple but oh-so striking, the vases can be purchased really cheaply from stores like IKEA and your local fruit market will net you a bargain on the fruit front.

Place settings – naturally!

Save money on printed place settings by channelling the seasons. For a spring wedding attach a feather to a small luggage label inscribed with the guest's name. If marrying in summer, paint your guests' names on beach pebbles. For autumn, collect large leaves, press them, and then write your guests' names on them in a gold or silver marker pen. And for winter sparkle, sprinkle glitter or frosting on the tips of fir cones. Write the guest's name on a piece of textured paper then slot it between the prickles.

Booked up

Use old hardback books, bought cheaply in bulk from jumble sales or from auction sites, as unusual centrepieces and then title your tables after famous love stories – *Gone with the Wind*, *Wuthering Heights* and *Cinderella*!

Be seated

Seating plans can be designed and printed on a home computer or, if you've a talent for calligraphy, by hand. Whichever you choose, leave it until the last possible minute, as inevitably someone will be poorly and will be a no-show.

Feathered friends

Collect feathers on walks or buy coloured feathers from craft shops and display in vases for a striking focal point for your tables.

Take a bow

Instead of napkin rings, simply tie big bows around your napkins with ribbon that complements your colour scheme.

Comedy props

By each table have a small box of comedy props: fake moustaches, eye patches, daft glasses, feather boas – let your imagination run amok. Leave a note asking guests to use the props for their own table's photo shoot. This can be a great ice-breaker for people who are seated together but who don't know each other so well.

GET THE PARTY STARTED

♥♥♥♥♥♥♥♥

43 A WARM RECEPTION

So, you have your venue, you will have tied the knot, posed for pics and the speeches will be done and dusted. Time to get down to the serious business of partying! But when you are planning your entertainment, give some thought to the practicalities. The first thing to investigate is the restrictions and equally the flexibility of your room or venue. Is there a dance floor? Will you have space to create a seating area away from the music? Is the party element of proceedings going to kick in at a specific time – to coincide with the arrival of evening guests, for example? Early planning is essential in this area so do consider your reception as soon as you can – what you want from your reception could dictate the sort of venue you need to consider, so you'll need to do some joined-up thinking and be willing to compromise in order to manage your budget effectively.

If you're looking at having some form of entertainment in the afternoon as well as in the evening, think about your own playlist going out on an MP3 player or iPod (see tip 44) in the afternoon, which saves money but gives you a musical backdrop while people are eating. And if you're having afternoon tea, then you can throw in some 'Tea for Two' style numbers to dovetail with the theme.

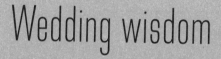

Wedding wisdom

'For the evening we had a disco hosted by my music-loving cousin but in the afternoon our best man organised a family game show between our two families. It was a lot of fun and everyone got involved.'

Elizabeth

44 RAVE, REVUE OR TEA DANCE?

Celebrating your marriage with a party is a natural thing to want to do, but depending on your guest list it can be tricky to get the balance right and to host a party that suits all ages. One of the simplest solutions is to have a more sedate celebration following your meal, then a livelier 'do' later in the evening. This, of course, presumes that you are not marrying in the late afternoon so if you are, then you'll need to think carefully about the sort of reception that will work for you – and then balance it with your budget.

Weddings discos can be very cheesy, but there again cheesy can be easily embraced by everyone – who doesn't hit the floor for 'Mamma Mia' or 'YMCA'? But rather than pay for a mobile disco, put together your own playlist and get one of your friends to act as your 'Wheels of Steel' frontman. You might need to hire a couple of speakers and some lights, but otherwise an iPod stuffed with all your favourite tunes is all you need to get this party started.

Likewise, if you want some background music earlier in the day, to accompany your meal perhaps, then your own song or music selection adds a really personal touch to proceedings and is cheaper than hiring musicians.

A live band in the evening can be great fun, but unless you know someone who is in a band and who can do this for you at 'mates rates', it will be an additional expense.

Hiring a karaoke machine can also be a giggle, although if you can count a talented pianist (who has their own portable digital piano) amongst your friends, save the hire fee and ask them if they'll come and play for people who want to do their party pieces. Likewise, if you know someone who teaches dance, ask them to prepare a 'wedding routine' and then get them to teach it to the assembled company.

45 CHILD'S PLAY

Hiring magicians or entertainment for your smaller guests' reception can really whack out your budget, but children will get bored with nothing to do except listen to boring grown-up chatter, so make sure you cater for them. If there is a secure adjoining room, then you could consider setting up a portable DVD player and leaving a selection of films for wee ones to enjoy, or perhaps a big box of Lego (borrowed from a friend). Offer an older teenager a few pounds for staying with the smaller children.

Game on

A great family-friendly option is to place old-fashioned games on each table – Shut the Box, Buckaroo, dominoes, Ker-Plunk, etc. One bride who married during an extremely soggy March did this and reports that even when the sun came out in the afternoon, nobody bothered to go outside as the entire wedding party was involved in a highly competitive game of Trivial Pursuit!

Shh! Artist at work!

Print pictures to colour in from the Internet (see if you can find some of wedding scenes) and give these, along with pencils or crayons, to the little ones in your wedding party just before the speeches – give a prize for the best picture coloured by the quietest child!

Note: If you provide felt-tips, make sure they are the washable kind. Kids in best clothes and indelible ink won't endear you to parents.

Whizz quiz kidz
Prepare a special wedding day quiz for small people to fill out based on the wedding itself.

Peggy Sue got married
Old-fashioned wooden pegs can be bought cheaply from craft shops. Leave a box containing pipe cleaners (for arms!), scraps of fabric and some glue on the children's table and tell them to make their own bride and groom – give a prize for the best effort.

Once upon a time
Bring a selection of books to suit the various age ranges of the children who will be attending and invite them to use the special Wedding Library.

Ted 'n' toy
When you send out the invites include one especially for each child, asking them to bring two things: their best bear, dressed in his wedding togs, and a small and quiet toy. This way all the children can play swapsies when they get bored with their own.

46 BE OUR GUEST

A guest book does give you a beautiful record of who attended your special day, but why not get creative with your own version...?

You can either make your own book to reflect the theme of your wedding, or go for an alternative means of gathering people's thoughts and wishes.

If you want to stick with the traditional guest book, look at buying a reasonably priced hardback book containing plain paper. You can then customise it by creating a jacket to match your invitations or trimming with lace and ribbons to match the colour scheme of your day. Pre-press flowers that will appear in your bouquet to decorate the pages or, if you're artistic, create cartoons on the pages – such as caricatures of your friends with a speech bubble waiting for their comment.

Another idea is to have a scrapbook and ask guests to bring along a postcard that most represents how they feel about you as a couple to stick in with their messages.

Sentiment cards are a creative alternative. All you need is a stack of postcards and a receptacle to be used as a 'postbox'. Decorate the cards to your specifications and then leave a pile on each table, along with a selection of pens and a written request asking guests to sign the cards and add an apt quotation, a wish for your future happiness, a drawing or a piece of advice for a happy marriage.

Another option, if you or anyone you know can claim embroidery as a skill, is to ask guests to sign a tablecloth (embroidery marker pens are available from haberdashery counters) and then embroider the signatures and messages at a later date. Buy your cloth or cover cheaply online or use an existing item, maybe something hidden in the depths of your linen cupboard. It's a fiddly job, but if you are a demon seamstress the embroidered names look stunning.

HAPPILY
EVER AFTER

♥♥♥♥♥♥♥♥

47 SO LONG, FAREWELL

Planning your exit from your reception might sound daft, but there are practical matters that need attending to. If you don't need to make a swift getaway to the airport, then you can be among the last of the revellers, but you will still need to have planned your transport back home or to wherever you will be spending your wedding night (unless you are staying at your reception venue). By asking a friend, in advance of the wedding, if they will be able to act as your taxi driver, you will save money on a 'real' taxi.

If you are heading off on honeymoon directly, make sure that you have a checklist that you can tick off before you leave. Some of the mistakes made by newly-weds who waltz out of their reception and head for the honeymoon hills can be alarmingly expensive. House keys forgotten can result in a less than warm welcome home – in the shape of a bill from a locksmith. Passports left behind, necessitating an emergency taxi to collect and deliver the missing documents to the airport, is another.

Make sure that you have paid everyone who needs to be paid. Make one of your nearest and dearest responsible for this task, giving them cash in advance of the event along with a list of who is due what. It might not save you money but it certainly saves any ill feeling on the part of anyone who might feel that they had been forgotten.

If the bride is changing out of her wedding dress, then it should be entrusted to someone she can depend upon to ensure that it is taken home, to the cleaners or back to the hire shop. With the latter you could incur a penalty fee for not returning the garment on time, which is hard to do if you're in Turkey and your frock is in the boot of your matron of honour's car.

Just Married

Wedding wisdom

'Our best wedding deal was a free honeymoon, thanks to winning a competition on our local radio station! There's lots of wedding competitions if you start looking for them – just put "win a wedding" into a search engine and see what comes up.'

Christopher

48 AND SO TO BED

If you are holding your reception at a hotel then there should be special rates for the wedding party, often with the honeymoon suite thrown in. If you can book all the rooms, then you should qualify for a discount here too. And negotiate for not just the best price, but also for upgrades: free breakfast; a bottle of bubbly in your room; complimentary spa treatments for the bride and groom. If you are booking a wedding and/or reception, then you'll be giving a hotel a good chunk of business. This means you have bargaining power, so be sure to use it, albeit politely!

If you are going elsewhere for your wedding night do make sure that you let staff know in advance that you will have just married. You may well find that a basket of fruit or a bottle of wine is waiting for you on arrival.

Finally, if you're going home, make sure that your first night of wedded bliss is special (steady!) by having your bed made up with new bedding that you haven't paid a penny for. Ask family to buy this as a wedding present and to give it to you in advance of the big day. Crisp and new, when you finally fall into bed after what has hopefully been the happiest day of your life, your bedding will be the perfect representation of your newly-wed status.

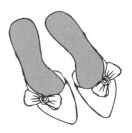

Wedding wisdom

'We knew from the outset that we wanted to have a fantastic honeymoon and to do this we knew we would have to compromise on the actual wedding. By really scrutinising all the items on the list we were able to spend where it mattered and save where it didn't. We had an incredible day – and our dream honeymoon.'

Emma

49 THANK YOU VERY MUCH

Having used the skills and talents of your friends and family, and having delegated tasks to them, not to mention all the gifts you will have received, you will inevitably have a lot of thank yous to extend after your wedding. Try to do these as soon as possible afterwards and to send a thank you that will remind people of what an amazing day it was. Given that postage is expensive you can save money by making or sourcing your thank yous. You could:

- Send a home-made card that matches your invites.

- Make special 'thank you' notepaper with a simple photo of you both inserted at the top.

- If you are going on honeymoon, bulk buy cheap postcards of a local beauty spot and send these.

- If you have a good candid snap from your wedding, taken by a close friend or family, surf the Internet and compare deals on getting cards made out of it. There is almost always a company offering a special rate.

If you will be moving house directly after the wedding, double up your change of address cards as 'thank you' cards.

If you are marrying close to Christmas, slip your thank yous into your Christmas cards.

If you're creative, then make a sketch or a poem the focus of your 'thank you' note.

Top Tip!

Send a thank you that will remind people of what an amazing day it was.

50 HOST WITH THE POST

While it is now a dying trend to send out cake to people who couldn't come to your wedding, if you have cut down on the number of guests in order to reduce your costs then sending a piece of your wedding cake is a lovely way to gently remind people that you care about them – assuming that you had a cake.

Of course, the cheapest way to do this is to deliver cake to people in person, which, if they live locally, you should make an effort to do, ideally taking a few snaps of the day along with you. Or, invite your local friends and family to come and have tea with you and serve the cake along with some Earl Grey.

If you have to send cake by post, however, do make sure that it is well packaged. Boxes for the purpose can be purchased; easily your best bet is online auction sites, where end-of-line or leftover boxes from other weddings can be snapped up very cheaply.

Finally, don't forget to keep some back for you and yours. If you look as if you're going to run short, ask yourself this: who, apart from you, will know that what you pop into the box for posting isn't what was served at the wedding? Nip to your local supermarket for a cunning substitute.

If you're interested in finding out more about our gift
books, find us on Facebook at **Summersdale Publishers**
and follow us on Twitter: @Summersdale.

www.summersdale.com